WILD
WONDERS

Why Do Reptiles Have Scales?

And Other Questions About Evolution and Classification

PAT JACOBS

PowerKiDS press

Published in 2017 by
The Rosen Publishing Group, Inc.
29 East 21st Street, New York, NY 10010

Cataloging-in-Publication Data
Names: Jacobs, Pat.
Title: Why do reptiles have scales? / Pat Jacobs.
Description: New York : PowerKids Press, 2017. | Series: Wildlife wonders | Includes index.
Identifiers: ISBN 9781499432091 (pbk.) | ISBN 9781499432756 (library bound) | ISBN 9781508153399 (6 pack)
Subjects: LCSH: Reptiles--Juvenile literature. | Reptiles--Evolution--Juvenile literature.
Classification: LCC QL644.2 J33 2017 | DDC 597.9--d23

Series Editor: Julia Bird
Packaged by: Dynamo Limited

Picture credits
Key: **t**=top, **b**=bottom
Cover: fivespots/Shutterstock, Yongkiet Jitwattanatam/Shutterstock; p1 Yongkiet Jitwattanatam/Shutterstock; p4 **t** Mogens Trolle/Shutterstock, p4 **b** Catmando/Shutterstock; p5 **t** Andreas Meyer/Shutterstock, p5 **b** njaj/Shutterstock; p6 (sea snake) Rich Carey/Shutterstock, (elapid snake) Caleb Foster/Shutterstock, (viper) MF Photo/Shutterstock, (colubrid) Toni Genes/Shutterstock; p7 (boa) feathercollector/Shutterstock, (worm lizard) neil hardwick/Shutterstock; p8 **t** Mathee Suwannarak/Shutterstock, p8 **b** TFoxFoto/Shutterstock; p9 **t** arka38/Shutterstock, p9 **b** Cathy Keifer/Shutterstock; p10 **t** dirkr/Shutterstock, p10 **b** Becky Stares/Shutterstock; p11 **t** apiguide/Shutterstock, p11 **b** apiguide/Shutterstock; p12 **t** © Brian Bevan / ardea.com, p12 **b** © M. Watson / ardea.com; p13 **t** AlessandroZocc/Shutterstock, p13 **b** worldswildlifewonders/Shutterstock; p14 **t** IrinaK/Shutterstock, p14 **b** Sebastian Duda/Shutterstock; p15 **t** voylodyon/Shutterstock, p15 **b** Dynamo; p16 **t** Sergey Uryadnikov/Shutterstock, p16 **b** Cathy Keifer/Shutterstock; p17 **t** Cathy Keifer/Shutterstock, p17 **b** Dynamo; p18 **t** Lorraine Swanson/Shutterstock, p18 **b** Heiko Kiera/Shutterstock; p19 **t** orlandin/Shutterstock, p19 **b** David Evison/Shutterstock; p20 **t** Mike Price/Shutterstock, p20 **b** Michael J Thompson/Shutterstock; p21 **t** IrinaK/Shutterstock, p21 **b** Marietjie/Shutterstock; p22 **t** kkaplin/Shutterstock, p22 **b** feathercollector/Shutterstock; p23 **t** Matt Jeppson/Shutterstock, p23 **b** Photo Fun/Shutterstock; p24 **t** tratong/Shutterstock, p24 **b** Alberto Loyo/Shutterstock; p25 **t** Sergey Uryadnikov/Shutterstock, p25 **b** fivespots/Shutterstock; p26 **t** Leo Shoot/Shutterstock, p26 **b** fivespots/Shutterstock; p27 **t** fivespots/Shutterstock, p27 **b** ACEgan/Shutterstock; p28 **t** MarclSchauer/Shutterstock, p28 **b** Cameramannz/Shutterstock; p29 **t** 8155069152/Shutterstock, p29 **b** Natursports/Shutterstock; p30 **t** Audrey Snider-Bell/Shutterstock, p30 **b** edography/Shutterstock

Manufactured in the United States of America
CPSIA Compliance Information: Batch #BW17PK: For Further Information contact Rosen Publishing, New York, New York at 1-800-237-9932.

Contents

Words in **bold** can be found in the glossary on page 31.

What is a reptile?

Reptiles were the first **vertebrates** to become fully **adapted** to life on dry land. They are cold-blooded animals, which means that their body temperature changes according to their surroundings. A reptile's skin is covered with scales made of keratin, the same material as our hair and nails.

Reptiles cannot control their body temperature. They bask in the Sun to warm up and move into the shade when they get too hot.

Dinosaurs (see box text) included the largest animals ever to have walked the Earth.

Ruling reptiles

Reptiles **evolved** more than 300 million years ago from reptile-like amphibians. Amphibians have moist skin and breed in water. Reptiles developed tough, scaly skin and eggs with tough shells, so they could move away from the water and spread throughout the world. They became so successful that giant reptiles, including dinosaurs and pterosaurs, ruled the Earth during the **Mesozoic era**.

Winged lizards

Pterosaurs were flying reptiles that lived alongside the dinosaurs. They were the earliest vertebrates to develop powered flight. Their wings were made up of skin and muscle and stretched from their ankles to their extra-long fourth finger.

With a wingspan of about 36 feet (11 m), the pterosaur Quetzalcoatlus was one of the largest flying animals of all time.

Marine giants

While dinosaurs ruled the land during the Mesozoic era, other reptiles took to the water. During the **Cretaceous period**, marine monsters, including the fearsome mosasaurs, **preyed** on fish, birds and other reptiles.

Mosasaurs stalked their prey until it was within striking distance of their massive jaws.

Classification of reptiles

The main groups of reptiles are turtles, crocodilians, snakes, lizards and tuataras. Snakes and legless lizards look similar but they are different. Lizards have eyelids and ear openings, unlike snakes, and a lizard's tail makes up two thirds of its length, while a snake's makes up just a third.

Turtles

Turtles, tortoises and terrapins are among the oldest of today's reptiles. They have hardly changed since they first appeared more than 220 million years ago.

Crocodilians

Crocodilians include alligators, crocodiles, gharials and caimans. They first appeared about 84 million years ago and are the closest living relatives of the birds.

Colubrids

About two-thirds of all snakes belong to the colubrid family. Most are not **venomous.** They live on every continent except Antarctica.

Vipers

Vipers are venomous snakes that are found in the Americas, Africa, Europe and Asia. They include rattlesnakes and adders. They have long, hinged **fangs**. Most give birth to live young.

Elapid snakes

Elapids are a family of agile, venomous snakes, which live in warm parts of the world. They include the king cobra and some tree-dwelling and burrowing snakes.

Sea snakes

These elapid snakes have adapted to life in salt water. They have evolved paddle-like tails and have a **gland** that gets rid of excess salt. Some have the strongest venom of all snakes.

Boas

Boas are non-venomous **constrictor** snakes found in America, Africa, Europe, Asia and some Pacific islands. Females are usually larger than males and they give birth to live young.

Pythons

Pythons live in Africa and Asia. They are non-venomous constrictor snakes that lay eggs. The reticulated python is the longest known snake.

Iguanas

Iguanas are plant-eating lizards that live in tropical regions. They have good eyesight and are well **camouflaged**. Marine iguanas are found only on the Galápagos Islands.

Chameleons

Chameleons are lizards that are well known for their ability to change color. Most live in trees. Those **species** that live on the ground usually have brown skin for camouflage.

Geckos

Thanks to their sticky feet, geckos can walk up walls and hang from ceilings. These lizards communicate with one another using chirping sounds. **Nocturnal** geckos have excellent night vision.

Monitors

Monitor lizards have long necks, strong legs and powerful claws. They include the Komodo dragon, the largest lizard alive today.

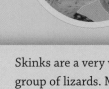

Skinks

Skinks are a very varied group of lizards. Most have small legs and no obvious neck. Some have lost their forelegs completely and look more like snakes.

Anguid lizards

This group includes alligator lizards and several species of legless lizards, including slow worms and glass lizards. Some lay eggs and others give birth to live young.

Worm lizards

Worm lizards are burrowers and have adapted to a life spent almost entirely underground. Three of the four groups have lost all traces of legs.

Tuataras

Tuataras appeared about 220 million years ago. They were once widespread, but today only two species remain on a few islands in New Zealand.

Why do reptiles have scales?

Reptiles' scales keep water out and protect them from injury. Snakes use the scales on their belly to help them grip the ground as they slither along. Scutes are tougher, horny scales, which are found on the backs of crocodiles and alligators and on the shells of tortoises and turtles.

A tortoise's shell is covered with scutes. Its weight slows the tortoise down, but it provides excellent protection from predators.

Armor plating

Cuvier's dwarf caiman is the smallest living species of crocodilian. Perhaps to make up for its small size, it is covered in thick, sharp scutes. This body armor protects it from predators – including human hunters. Crocodilians are killed for their skins, which are made into leather, but Cuvier's dwarf caiman's armored skin is too thick so hunters leave it alone.

Cuvier's dwarf caiman lives in rivers and streams in South America, where it preys on fish and shellfish.

Changing color

Some species of chameleon have **pigments** beneath their scaly outer skin that move when they get a message from the animal's brain and make its skin change color. Some chameleons are darker in the morning, so they can absorb (take in) more heat. Others change color to hide from predators or to signal to **mates** or rivals.

Masters of disguise

Some geckos have specially adapted scales that blend into their surroundings so predators find them almost impossible to spot. A leaf-tailed gecko found in the forests of Madagascar looks just like twisted dried leaves, while the mossy leaf-tailed gecko has evolved moss- and bark-colored scales.

These two mossy leaf-tailed geckos are almost invisible as they hide on a tree trunk. They can even change color to match their surroundings.

9

Reptile habitats

Reptiles are cold-blooded, so their bodies do not produce heat by burning calories. This means that they need far less food than mammals of the same size. Reptiles can live in harsh habitats, such as the desert, where mammals and birds would struggle to survive.

The web-footed gecko lives in the desert and has evolved large feet to stop it sinking into the sand. It uses them to dig a burrow where it hides during the day.

Grasslands

These habitats are home to many snakes, lizards and tortoises. Most snakes and lizards are meat eaters and grasslands provide plenty of small mammal or insect prey. Tortoises are plant eaters, so a grassy habitat supplies them with all the food they need.

Slow worms live in meadows, woodlands and fields. They are burrowing lizards and eat slugs, snails, worms and small insects.

In the treetops

Lizards that live in trees have developed sharp claws for climbing. Tree-climbing snakes have long tails that coil around a branch and act like an anchor as the snake pulls itself up.

Iguanas spend most of their lives in the rain forest trees feeding on leaves, flowers and fruit.

Waterways

Some reptiles have adapted to spend most of their lives in the water. Crocodilians' eyes, ears and nostrils are on top of their head, so they can keep their body hidden while they wait for prey. A transparent extra eyelid protects their eye underwater and a flap of skin at the back of their throat keeps water out when they attack. Sea turtles have large lungs and special systems for storing and saving oxygen, so they can stay underwater for hours at a time.

Gharials move quickly in water, but their legs are not suited to walking on land, so they have to slide on their bellies. Their long, thin jaws and sharp teeth have evolved to catch fish.

Getting around

Most four-legged reptiles walk with their legs out to the side, rather than underneath their bodies like mammals. However, there are some species of lizards that can walk on two legs. The best known is the basilisk lizard, which darts across the water to escape danger.

The basilisk lizard has fringes of skin on its back feet. As it slaps them against the water, they create air pockets that stop it sinking.

Slithering and sidewinding

Snakes are thought to have evolved from a lizard that burrowed on land, or swam in the sea. As its legs became less useful, they shrank and eventually disappeared. Most snakes slither along by thrusting their bodies from side to side in a series of curves. Some species throw their bodies sideways when they travel across loose surfaces, such as sand. This is called sidewinding.

Sidewinder snakes fling their bodies sideways in an S shape. Most of the snake's body is off the ground as it moves.

Sticky feet

Geckos are able to cling to walls and ceilings because they have millions of tiny hairs on the bottom of their feet that are invisible to the naked eye. These produce electrical forces that glue the animals to almost any material, even glass. As the gecko walks, it rolls the hairs onto the surface, then peels them off again.

The ridges on a gecko's toes are made up of fine hairs, each of which branches into thousands of tiny tips.

Strong swimmers

Crocodilians, marine iguanas, sea snakes and turtles have all adapted to life in the water. Many snakes and lizards that normally live on land are excellent swimmers too. Sea turtles move slowly and awkwardly when they come ashore but, thanks to their **streamlined** shells and powerful front flippers, they can speed through the water at up to 18.6 miles per hour (30 km/h).

Sea turtles use their back feet for steering, like the rudder of a boat.

Senses and intelligence

Reptiles have good senses of sight and smell, but they are not known for their intelligence. However, a group of Puerto Rican anole lizards recently proved to be smarter than birds in a series of problem-solving tests.

Anole lizards have shown signs of intelligence. They quickly adapted their behavior to obtain a food reward in tests.

All-around vision

Chameleons judge range and distance better than any other reptile. Each of their eyes can move in a different direction, so one can look forwards while the other looks backwards. Some lizards and the lizard-like tuatara have a third eye, which looks like a tiny oval, on top of their head that can detect light, but not shapes.

Chameleons can look all around them when they are searching for prey.

Infrared detectors

Several families of snakes have evolved pit organs, which allow them to sense **infrared radiation** and "see" heat given off by other animals. This means they can locate warm-blooded predators and prey, even when they are hidden. It may also help them to find warmer and cooler places so they can keep their body temperature constant.

Rattlesnakes belong to the pit viper family, named after their pit organs (circled). These help them to hunt at night.

Tasting the air

When a snake or lizard wants to smell something it flicks out its tongue, then presses the tips of its tongue against two pits in the roof of its mouth. These pits detect tiny particles from the air and help the snake or lizard stalk its prey or find a mate. They are part of the Jacobson's organ, which exists in some other animals, but is especially well developed in reptiles.

brain

Jacobson's organ

tongue

pits

tongue

Snakes and some lizards have evolved forked tongues, so the tips can touch the two pits of the Jacobson's organ. The deeper the fork in the tongue, the more the reptile relies on this organ.

Finding food

Most reptiles are ambush predators. They lie in wait until their prey comes within reach, then strike with lightning speed. Crocodilians often lurk close to the water's edge, ready to attack any animal that comes to drink.

*Thousands of wildebeests cross the Mara river during their annual **migration**, so crocodiles lie in wait near the riverbank, ready to strike.*

Turbo-charged tongue

A chameleon's tongue shoots out of its mouth at 33 feet (10 m) per second. Powerful muscles fire the tongue forwards, while **lubricated** spaces reduce the **friction** between the muscles and bones. The round tip is covered with sticky saliva and can seize prey in as little as 0.07 seconds.

Chameleons are slow-moving creatures but they have super fast tongues, which are up to twice the length of their bodies.

Fishing lure

The alligator snapping turtle moves too slowly to chase its food, so it waits on the riverbed with its mouth wide open to reveal its pink-tipped tongue. This looks like a small worm and lures fish and other prey within striking distance of the turtle's snapping jaws.

When fish, frogs, shellfish or other turtles are lured within reach of the alligator snapping turtle's jaws, it swallows them whole or slices them in half.

tongue

Big meal

Most snakes eat other animals, but the egg-eating snake has evolved to eat birds' eggs. Snakes have very flexible jaws and stretchy bodies, so they can eat things that are far larger than their heads. As the egg moves down the snake's neck, bony spines break the shell. The snake swallows the contents of the egg and spits out the shell.

Egg-eating snakes are good climbers and have an excellent sense of smell, so they can tell whether an egg is rotten before they swallow it.

Reproduction

Many reptiles behave in a special way to signal that they are ready to mate. Some lizards change color and bob their heads, male turtles stroke a female's face with their flippers and male Nile crocodiles slap their heads on the water, bellow and squirt water out of their nostrils.

*When a female garter snake comes out of **hibernation**, she releases a scent that attracts nearby males. They form a squirming ball as they all battle to mate with her.*

Laying eggs

Reptiles usually lay their eggs in a hole, or scrape, in the ground. Most reptiles leave the eggs to hatch on their own, but pythons and cobras coil themselves around their eggs to keep them warm. Crocodiles guard their nests and sometimes help the babies out of their eggs by gently biting through the shells.

The shells of reptiles' eggs are tough and leathery. Baby reptiles, such as this python, have a special egg tooth to tear a hole in the shell.

Live birth

Most reptiles lay eggs, but some give birth to live young and the number appears to be increasing as a result of evolution. This may be because loss of habitat has forced more reptiles to move to colder regions, where temperatures fall too low for eggs to hatch. Scientists believe up to 100 types of reptiles that once laid eggs now give birth to live babies.

The common lizard lives as far north as the Arctic Circle. In these cold areas it gives birth to live young.

Boy or girl?

The temperature of certain reptiles' eggs during the **incubation** period affects the sex of the **hatchlings**. In the case of Nile crocodiles, if the temperature in the nest is between 89°F (31.7°C) and 94°F (34.5°C) the babies will all be male; if it is above or below, they will all be female. The temperature of the nest also changes the sex of turtle babies.

If the temperature in this green turtle nest is high, all the hatchlings will be female. If it is cooler, they will all be male.

Growing up

Baby reptiles look like miniature adults and are able to feed themselves straight away. However, they are at great risk of attack by predators and many are eaten during their first few months. Those that survive can go on to live long lives. Saltwater crocodiles may live for 70 years and some turtles and tortoises can reach 100 years old.

Giant tortoises have a lifespan of 100 years or more.

Caring crocodilians

Crocodilians are the best reptile parents. The female buries her eggs in a mound of loose earth and both the male and female guard the nest until the babies signal that they are ready to hatch by making a chirping sound. The mother carefully removes the earth to expose the eggs, then gently carries the hatchlings to the water in her mouth.

Crocodilians protect their babies for several months until they are large enough to take care of themselves.

Going it alone

Female sea turtles come ashore and lay up to 200 eggs in the sand, then cover them and return to the sea. The baby turtles emerge about two months later. They have evolved to hatch at night, when there are fewer predators about, and head straight for the water. Female turtles will return to land about five years later to lay their own eggs, but males will never come ashore again.

Turtle hatchlings face many predators including crabs, birds, raccoons and fish.

Shedding skin

Young reptiles grow quickly but their scaly skin does not grow with them. They shed, or lose, their skin as they grow. A snake's old skin usually comes off in one piece, but lizards often lose theirs in patches. Some lizards pull the old skin off with their mouth and eat it. Crocodilians and tortoises usually shed single scales or scutes, which are replaced by larger, thicker scales.

Snakes shed their skins several times a year. As well as allowing them to grow, shedding the old skin gets rid of parasites.

Self-defense

Many reptiles avoid predators by blending in with their surroundings. If they are confronted, some have developed special tricks to confuse or frighten an attacker.

When a frilled lizard is threatened, it hisses and opens the large skin flap around its head.

Coming or going?

The stump-tailed skink's tail is full of fat, which keeps the lizard alive during its winter hibernation. The oversized tail looks just like its head and, for this reason, it is also known as the two-headed skink. Predators do not know which end of the lizard to attack and their confusion gives the skink a chance to make its escape.

The stump-tailed skink has a heavily armored body, covered with large, rough scales.

Secret weapon

If the short-horned lizard's spiky skin is not enough to deter an attacker, it has two other tricks to make a predator think twice. It can inflate its body so its sharp spines look even bigger and squirt blood from its eyes.

Short-horned lizards can squirt blood up to 10 feet (3 m) from the corners of their eyes!

Shedding a tail

Some lizards can also shed their tail if a predator seizes it. The tail keeps on wriggling, which distracts the attacker while the lizard runs away. The tail regrows, but it will be shorter than the original.

This lizard's tail has regrown after the original was shed, but it does not look exactly the same.

Fearsome beasts

Nile crocodiles live close to humans and are estimated to kill about 200 people a year.

Humans have evolved to be afraid of snakes, which may have helped them to survive in earlier times. However, more people die each year from bee and wasp stings than from snakebites. The most dangerous reptiles are crocodiles, which are responsible for more attacks on humans than any other.

Lethal squeeze

Constrictor snakes, such as boas, anacondas and pythons, grab their prey with their small, hooked teeth, then wrap their muscular bodies around their victim and gradually tighten the coils until it dies from a heart attack or suffocation. It can take hours for a snake to swallow large prey and days for the meal to be digested.

This python has captured a small gazelle. After such a huge meal, the snake will not need to eat again for several months.

Dangerous dragons

Komodo dragons ambush large animals such as deer, wild pigs and water buffalo and seize them in their powerful jaws. Their prey might escape, but the dragon's saliva is full of **bacteria** that kill their victim several days later. The dragon uses its excellent sense of smell to stalk the dying creature, ready to devour it when it collapses.

The Komodo dragon is a type of monitor lizard. It can grow to 10 feet (3 m) long, making it the world's largest lizard.

Deadly bite

Venom has evolved in animals from jellyfish to scorpions. Venomous snakes have developed their own cocktails of poison, which they inject into their prey through hollow fangs. The Gila (pronounced "Heela") monster and its cousin, the Mexican beaded lizard, are among a handful of venomous lizards.

Instead of injecting venom through fangs, Gila monsters have large, grooved teeth in their lower jaw that carry venom into the bite.

Remarkable reptiles

The time when reptiles ruled the world may have passed, but those that have evolved since the time of the dinosaurs are equally amazing.

The tokay gecko becomes lighter or darker to blend in with its surroundings. It is dark gray with orange-red spots in daylight and light gray with bluish spots at night.

World-class sprinters

Monitor lizards are thought to have evolved from marine reptiles called mosasaurs (see page 5) and they differ from other lizards in several ways. They have a higher **metabolic rate** than most reptiles and are active hunters. Their excellent eyesight and ability to run very fast over long distances enables them to catch prey such as rabbits.

Most lizards cannot run and breathe at the same time, but monitor lizards are exceptions to this rule. This helps them to move more quickly – some can run 25 miles per hour (40 km/h).

Monster snakes

Reticulated pythons are the world's longest snakes and regularly reach up to 23 feet (7 m) in length. Huge snakes have evolved at various times since the **extinction** of the dinosaurs, but a gigantic relative of today's boas and anacondas, which lived 60 million years ago, would have dwarfed them all. Called *Titanoboa*, this snake was 49 feet (15 m) long, weighed more than 1.1 tons (1 mt), and swallowed crocodiles whole.

Reticulated pythons live in tropical rain forests.

Deep divers

Leatherbacks are the world's largest turtles. They are the only remaining species of a family that dates back more than 100 million years. While other sea turtles have hard shells made of scutes, the leatherback's is made of thick, rubbery skin. Leatherbacks are one of the deepest diving marine animals thanks to adaptations including a streamlined shell, blood that holds a good supply of oxygen and a layer of fat, which keeps the turtle warm in cold water.

The leatherback's huge flippers power the turtle through the water at up to 22 miles per hour (35 km/h). It can reach depths of 4,200 feet (1, 280 m) and stay down for up to 85 minutes.

Reptiles at risk

Nearly a fifth of the world's estimated 10,000 species of reptiles are thought to be at risk of extinction, mainly from habitat loss due to farming and logging. Half of all freshwater turtles are threatened because they are caught for food and as pets. For many species, **captive breeding** programs are their only hope.

The Roti snake-necked turtle from Indonesia was first discovered in 1994. By 2000, so many had been caught to sell as pets that it came close to extinction.

Tuataras under threat

Tuataras live on just 30 small islands in New Zealand. As is the case with a number of reptiles, the temperature of the nest affects the sex of tuatara hatchlings. If it rises above 71.6°F (22°C), they will all be male. On one island there are already more male tuataras than females. It is feared that **global warming** will reduce the number of females so there are not enough to breed and that the future of these rare reptiles will be put at risk.

Tuataras are the only surviving members of a family of reptiles that lived during the time of the dinosaurs.

Python problem

Burmese pythons are making themselves at home in the Florida Everglades, after being released by pet owners or escaping from their enclosures. The snakes are breeding and the population is now estimated to be above 100,000. The constrictors prey on this sensitive habitat's rare and **endangered** species, including other reptiles.

This alligator in the Everglades finally won its ten-hour battle with a Burmese python by drowning the snake.

Unique lizards

Marine iguanas are the only lizards that live and feed in the sea. Scientists think that land-based iguanas drifted to the Galápagos Islands millions of years ago on a raft of debris. They evolved blunt snouts and sharp teeth to scrape **algae** off rocks, and flattened tails and spiky fins to help them swim. They have long, sharp claws for clinging to rocks and special glands that clean their blood of salt. They are threatened by pollution and by predators introduced by humans, such as wild dogs and cats.

Marine iguanas are at risk from predators when they bask on rocks to warm up after swimming in the cold water.

Awesome reptiles

Reptiles range from huge, deadly predators to tiny, jewel-like lizards. Here are just a few of the many fantastic facts about these cool creatures.

Small appetites

Because they are cold-blooded, reptiles need 30 to 50 times less food than birds and mammals (warm-blooded animals) of the same size.

Delayed reaction

A rattlesnake (below) can bite for up to an hour after it dies, even if its head has been cut off. Its **reflexes**, which can be triggered by its infrared sensors, remain active after death.

Tiny snake

The smallest snake is just 4 inches (10 cm) long and the width of a strand of spaghetti. The Barbados thread snake eats termites and lays a single large egg.

Insect incubator

To protect its eggs, the perentie monitor lizard lays them inside a termite mound. Termites carefully maintain the temperature and humidity of their nests and these conditions are perfect for perentie eggs.

Clever lizards

An experiment at San Diego Zoo proved that rock monitor lizards can count up to six. The monitors were offered different numbers of snails and knew when one or more was missing.

Mini chameleon

A chameleon recently discovered in Madagascar measures just 1.2 inches (3 cm) from nose to tail, but it is almost twice the size of the smallest known lizard, the Jaragua Sphaero, which measures a mere 0.6 inch (1.6 cm).

Strongest bite

Saltwater crocodiles (below) have the strongest bite in the animal kingdom, but the muscles for opening the jaw are very weak, so their mouths can be held shut with a strong rubber band.

Glossary

Adapt To adjust to new conditions

Algae Simple organisms that grow in water

Bacteria Tiny life-forms. Some cause disease (we call these germs) and others are useful

Camouflage Natural coloring that allows an animal to blend in with its surroundings

Captive breeding Breeding animals in zoos, wildlife parks or other controlled habitats

Constrictor A snake that coils around its prey and squeezes it to death

Cretaceous period The last part of the Mesozoic era, 145–66 million years ago, which ended when the dinosaurs died

Endangered At risk of dying out completely

Evolve To develop gradually over generations

Extinction When all living members of a species have died out

Fang A long, sharp tooth

Friction Two surfaces rubbing together

Gland An organ in the body that produces chemicals, which are used in the body or released into the surroundings

Global warming An increase in the temperature of the Earth's atmosphere, thought to be caused by human activity

Hatchling A creature that has just hatched

Hibernation Going into a deep sleep to survive the cold weather when food is scarce

Incubation Keeping eggs warm until they are ready to hatch

Infrared radiation Rays of heat given off by a warm or hot object

Lubricate To make surfaces slippery so they slide against one another without friction

Mate One of a pair of animals that produce young together, or to produce young

Mesozoic era The time between 252 and 66 million years ago when the dinosaurs lived

Metabolic rate The speed at which the body burns food to produce energy

Migration Moving from one area to another according to the seasons, usually to find food

Nocturnal Active during the night

Parasite An animal that lives in or on another creature and feeds on that creature or on its food

Pigment Natural color in animal skin

Predator An animal that hunts other creatures for food

Prey To hunt other creatures for food, or an animal that is hunted by another for food

Reflexes An automatic action that is performed without thought

Species A group of animals that can breed with one another and produce healthy babies, which are able to breed when they grow up

Streamlined Shaped to move easily through air or water

Venomous Creatures that inject a poisonous liquid into their victims

Vertebrate An animal with a backbone

Index

Websites

PowerKids Press has developed an online list of websites related to the subject of this book. This site is updated regularly. Please use this link to access the list:

www.powerkidslinks.com/ww/reptiles